Collins
Spanish
Club

FUN, ACTIVE LEARNING

Book 1

Lucy Henry

Ruth Sharp & Rosi McNab

First published in 2009 by Collins
an imprint of HarperCollins Publishers
77–85 Fulham Palace Road
London w6 8jb

www.collinslanguage.com

9 8 7 6 5 4 3 2 1 0

A catalogue record for this book is available
from the British Library

Authors: Ruth Sharp and Rosi McNab
Illustrator: Mel Sharp
Designers: Rob Payne and Heike Schüssler

ISBN: 978-0-00-728758-1

CD recording by Talking Issues
Music by Myra Barretto and Daniel Murguialday
Actors: Elena Pavan Macías, Victoria Galache-Brown,
Alex Winslow Parsons and Ainara Campo
Printed in China through
Golden Cup Printing Services

Contents

1. **En el zoo** At the zoo 2
Introduction to Spanish pronunciation

2. **¿Cuántos?** How many? 6
Numbers 0-10 and some pronunciation rules

3. **Colorear** Colouring in 10
Colours, adjective agreement, possessive 'my' and word order

4. **Mi aspecto** My appearance 14
Describing appearances and practice of adjectives

5. **¡Feliz cumpleaños!** Happy birthday! 18
Numbers beyond ten, months of the year and talking about age

6. **¿Qué hora es?** What time is it? 21
Telling the time, days of the week and daily routine

7. **De pies a cabeza** From head to toe 24
Parts of the body

8. **Mi ropa** My clothes 28
Clothes, the circus and revision of word gender

9. **Mi habitación** My bedroom 36
An introduction to prepositions *in*, *on* and *under*

10. **Mis cosas** My things 40
School equipment and the Spanish alphabet

Resumen Summary 44

Answer key 46

EN EL ZOO

1. At the zoo

Help your child: This unit is all about zoo animals, with a gentle introduction to the idea of word gender. Since the concept of masculine/feminine words doesn't exist in English, it may take time for your child to understand. With this in mind, the topic of word gender will be revisited throughout the book. Also in this unit are some pronunciation tips. Have fun listening to the CD with your child and, together, try to copy the pronunciation.

¡Vamos al zoo!
Let's go to the zoo!

Escucha y canta
Listen and sing

Track 1

En el zoo estoy.
I'm at the zoo.

¿Qué animales ves hoy?
What animals do you see today?

Veo un canguro.
I see a kangaroo.

Un canguro. ¿Y qué más?
A kangaroo. And what else?

Y nada más.
And nothing else.

En el zoo estoy.
¿Qué animales ves hoy?
Veo un canguro, una jirafa.
Un canguro, una jirafa. ¿Y qué más?
Y nada más.

En el zoo estoy...

UN CANGURO

UNA JIRAFA

UN CHIMPANCÉ

UN ELEFANTE

UNA TORTUGA

UN COCODRILO

¿Qué animal es? Escucha y participa

Which animal is it? Listen and join in

Track 2

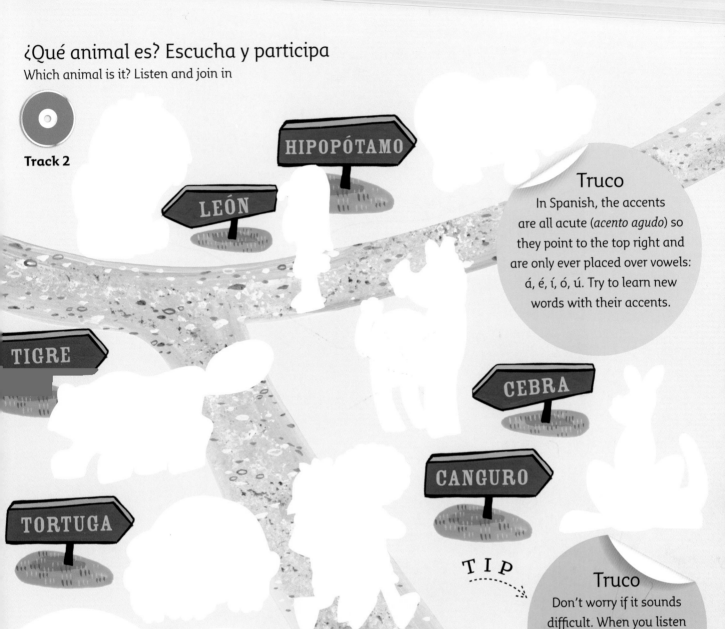

HIPOPÓTAMO

LEÓN

TIGRE

CEBRA

CANGURO

TORTUGA

Truco
In Spanish, the accents are all acute (*acento agudo*) so they point to the top right and are only ever placed over vowels: á, é, í, ó, ú. Try to learn new words with their accents.

TIP

Truco
Don't worry if it sounds difficult. When you listen to the CD you'll learn which part of the word to stress.

¡El detective!

Did you notice?

There are accents in the words *león*, *chimpancé* and *hipopótamo*. Spanish and English words are split up into syllables. In English, the word 'elephant' has 3 syllables (<u>e</u>-le-phant) and the first one is stressed. In Spanish, *elefante* has 4 syllables (e-le-<u>fan</u>-te) and the third one is stressed. Generally the second last syllable is stressed in Spanish:

    can-<u>gu</u>-ro   co-co-<u>dri</u>-lo

If there is an accent, it tells us to stress a different part of the word:

    not   *chim-<u>pan</u>-ce*   but   *chim-pan-<u>cé</u>*

Practise saying the names of the animals slowly and stressing the correct syllable. Count the syllables on your fingers.

    ji-<u>ra</u>-fa   *e-le-<u>fan</u>-te*   *<u>ti</u>-gre*   *le-<u>ón</u>*   *chim-pan-<u>cé</u>*

¿Qué animal es? Rellena los huecos con las letras que faltan
Which animal is it? Fill in the missing letters

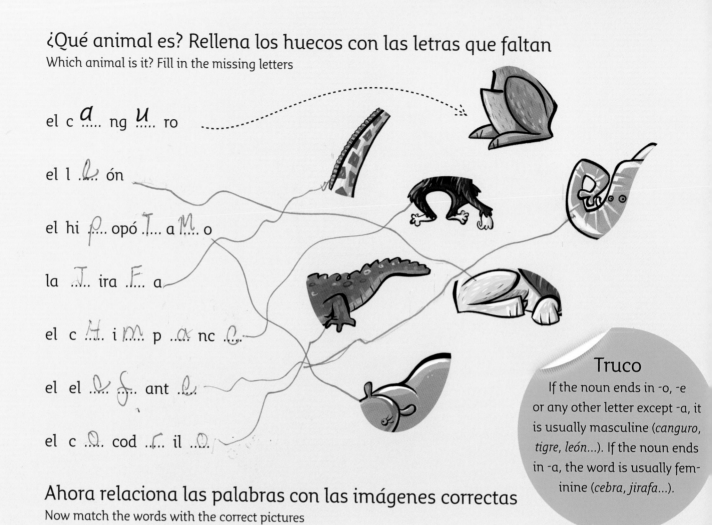

el c *a* ng *u* ro

el l *e* ón

el hi *p* opó *T* a *M* o

la *J* ira *F* a

el c *H* i *M* p *a* nc *é*

el el *e* *f* ant *e*

el c *o* cod *r* il *o*

Ahora relaciona las palabras con las imágenes correctas
Now match the words with the correct pictures

Truco
If the noun ends in -o, -e or any other letter except -a, it is usually masculine (*canguro, tigre, león*...). If the noun ends in -a, the word is usually feminine (*cebra, jirafa*...).

¡El detective!

Did you notice?

Some words have *el* and some have *la* before them. They both mean 'the' but, in Spanish, nouns (naming words, like 'hippo', 'apple' or 'man') are either masculine or feminine. This is called gender. *El* goes before a masculine noun and *la* before a feminine noun.

Gender has nothing to do with whether the object is male or female. A male tortoise is still <u>*la* tortuga</u>, and a female chimpanzee is <u>*el* chimpancé</u>.

Relaciona los animales con "el" o "la"
Link the animals with *el* or *la*

elefante
cebra
canguro
león
tortuga

el   la

cocodrilo
chimpancé
jirafa
hipopótamo
tigre

Truco
Try to learn new words with *el* and *la*.

Sopa de letras: ¿Cuántos animales puedes encontrar?

Word search: How many animals can you find?

c	o	c	o	d	r	i	l	o
a	e	v	t	i	g	r	e	a
n	l	b	o	m	g	b	ó	d
g	j	i	r	a	f	a	n	c
u	z	n	t	a	h	f	q	v
r	e	l	e	f	a	n	t	e
o	d	t	o	r	t	u	g	a

✓ Perfecto

Truco
In Spanish, the letter h is always silent.

¡El detective!

Did you notice?

A lot of Spanish words look like English words but some letters are said in a different way.

To say the word *zoo* in Spanish, you pronounce the *z* like *th* in thumb. The letter *c* before *e* or *i* is pronounced in the same way.

The *j* in *jirafa* should sound like the *ch* in the Scottish word 'loch'. The letter *g* before *e* or *i* should sound the same.

Which is true? Underline the correct answer:

In Spanish...

1. *z* sounds like: a. the *z* in *zebra* b. the *th* in 'thirty'
2. a. *ce* and *ci* sound the same as the Spanish *z*
   b. *ca*, *co* and *cu* sound the same as the Spanish *z*
3. *j* sounds like: a. the *ch* in the Scottish word *loch* b. the *j* in *jam*
4. a. *ga*, *go* and *gu* sound the same as the Spanish *j*
   b. *ge* and *gi* sound the same as the Spanish *j*

Practise saying these Spanish words: *zoo, chimpancé, cebra, jirafa*

¿CUÁNTOS?

2. How many?

Help your child: This unit introduces numbers and farm animals, with guidelines on plurals and pronunciation. Encourage your child to count things you see in and out of the house and to play around with words, making them into plurals. Sing and rap along with your child – the rhythm of the music will make all the difference to their memory.

¡Escucha y participa!
Listen and join in!

Track 3

0 cero	1 uno	2 dos	3 tres	4 cuatro	5 cinco

6 seis	7 siete	8 ocho	9 nueve	10 diez

Truco
In Spanish, the letter *v* sounds exactly the same as the letter *b*.

1 Un gato
2 Dos patos
3 Tres gallos
4 Cuatro caballos
5 Cinco perros
6 Seis conejos
7 Siete pollitos
8 Ocho burritos
9 Nueve vacas
10 Diez cabras
¡Vamos a la granja!
¡Todos a la granja!

Pega la pegatina correcta debajo de cada número
Stick the correct sticker under each number

7 **2** **6** **10** **5** **3**

siete dos seis diez cinco tres

¿Cuántos huesos hay? Cuenta los huesos y completa las palabras
How many bones are there? Count the bones and complete the words

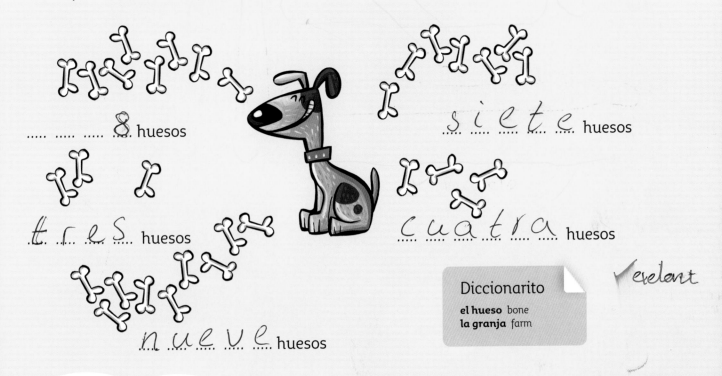

.... 8. huesos

s i e t e huesos

t r e s huesos

c u a t r o huesos

n u e v e huesos

Diccionarito
el hueso bone
la granja farm

✓exelant

¡El detective!
Did you notice?

When you listened to the CD you might have noticed that the *ll* in *gallo* and the *rr* in *burrito* are said differently to how they would be in English.

The *ll* in *gallo* is pronounced like the English *y* as in the word 'yoghurt'.

The *rr* in *burrito* should be rolled at the front of your mouth like a *purrrrring* cat. This sound can be difficult for English speakers – can you do it?

Which is true? Underline the correct answer:

In Spanish...

1. *ll* sounds like: a. the *ll* in 'yellow'   b. the *y* in 'yellow'
2. *rr* sounds like: a. the *r* in 'brrrr, it's cold!'   b. the *r* in *rug*

Purrrrrr. . . .

Pega las pegatinas correctas encima de las palabras
Stick the right stickers above the words

cuatro caballos

cinco perros

un gato

tres gallos

dos patos

Escribe las palabras debajo de las imágenes
Write the words under the pictures

nueve ....

siete ....

.... burritos

.... conejos

....

✓ Well Done!

¡El detective!
Did you notice?

The words *uno* (masculine) and *una* (feminine) mean 'a' or 'one'. *Un* is used before a masculine noun because it is easier to say.

el caballo   *la cabra*

un caballo   *una cabra*

¡Leerrrrrápido!

Speed reading!

Lee y di las palabras rápidamente
Read and say the words quickly

granja gato conejo jirafa

cebra cinco chimpancé cabra

pollo caballo cocodrilo gallo

Truco
One word is pronounced differently in each set. Can you see which it is?

¡El detective!

Did you notice?

There are lots of words that end with *-ito* and *-ita*. This is the Spanish way of saying something is small or cute. These endings can also be used to imply feelings of affection.

pollo (chicken) – *pollito* (chick)
burro (donkey) – *burrito* (little donkey)

The Spanish use these endings all the time so you'll hear it a lot if you go to Spain!

Truco
Try singing this song about different animals.

Canción: Escucha y canta
Song: Listen and sing

Track 4

Un elefante se balanceaba
One elephant balanced

Sobre la tela de una araña.
On a spider's web

Como veía que resistía
When he saw that it could hold him

Fue a llamar a otro elefante.
He called to another elephant.

Dos elefantes se balanceaban ...

Colorear

3. Colouring in

Help your child: In Spanish, some colour adjectives have to 'agree' with the word they are describing. This is a new concept for English speakers so don't worry if it seems difficult at first. In languages the mantra is *confidence breeds competence* - build your child's confidence in their spoken Spanish and they will soon be able to transfer this to all other aspects of the language.

Escucha y participa
Listen and join in

Track 5   ROJO   AZUL   VERDE   AMARILLO   MARRÓN

BLANCO   NEGRO   GRIS   ROSA   MORADO   NARANJA

Colorea los sombreros
Colour in the hats

un sombrero amarillo y rosa

un sombrero negro y naranja

un sombrero verde y marrón

una gorra morada y gris

una gorra azul y roja

Truco
In Spanish, they say 'a hat red' instead of 'a red hat'. A colour is an adjective (a describing word) and the word 'hat' is a noun (a naming word). In Spanish, the adjective usually comes after the noun.

Pega la cometa correcta en los espacios
Stick the correct kite in each space

CARLA   ANTONIO   PABLO MARTA   SOFÍA   MARCOS

Carla: "Mi cometa es roja y amarilla."

Antonio tiene una cometa azul y verde.

La cometa de Pablo es blanca y negra.

Marta: "Mi cometa es rosa y gris."

La cometa de Sofía es verde y roja.

Marcos tiene una cometa azul y amarilla.

¡El detective!
Did you notice?

Mi and *mis* both mean 'my'. *Mi* refers to one thing and
mis to more than one.

    mi cometa (my kite)   *mis cometas* (my kites)

Dibuja y colorea tu propia cometa
Draw and colour in your own kite

Completa la frase
Complete the sentence

Mi cometa es ....

As all *things* (nouns) in Spanish are either masculine or feminine, the colour that describes them often has to be made to look masculine or feminine too:

masculine	feminine
un sombrero roj**o**	una cometa roj**a**
un sombrero amarill**o**	una cometa amarill**a**
un sombrero blanc**o**	una cometa blanc**a**
un sombrero negr**o**	una cometa negr**a**

But only the colours that end in –o change to –a when describing a feminine word. The words *azul* (blue), *verde* (green), *gris* (grey), *marrón* (brown), *naranja* (orange) and *rosa* (pink) don't change – they are always the same whether they're describing a masculine or a feminine word.

un sombrero azul   *una cometa azul*

Escribe el color correcto en el espacio
Write the correct colour in the space

 una manzana ....

 un elefante ....

 una jirafa ....

 un sombrero ....

 una mariposa ....

 un gato ....

¡El detective!
Did you notice?

Just as colours change to look feminine or masculine, they also have to adapt to be plural. In this case, you add an –s (or sometimes –es).

*un sombrero roj**o***   *una cometa roj**a***
*dos sombreros roj**os***   *dos cometas roj**as***

El arco iris
The rainbow

Escucha y canta. Después colorea el arco iris
Listen and sing. Then colour in the rainbow

Track 6

ROJO NARANJA AMARILLO VERDE AZUL MORADO ROSA

Escribe un poema
Write a poem

If you can't think of any Spanish words to use, why not look on the internet? At www.collinslanguage.com there is a dictionary to help you. Type in an English word and it will tell you how you say it in Spanish!

Or you can use the words in the *diccionarito* below.

Truco
When you just say the colour, you don't need to change the ending. It only changes when it comes *after* the word it is describing: *blanco como la nieve* but *la nieve blanca.*

Negro como   *la noche* ....

Truco
Think about whether you should use 'the' or 'a' with each word you choose. Then use the correct *el, la, un* or *una.*

Blanco como   ....

Rojo como   ....

Azul como   ....

Amarillo como   ....

Verde como   ....

Diccionarito
la noche night
la nieve snow
el mar sea
el sol sun
la hoja leaf
este this
el tomate tomato

Mi Aspecto

4. My appearance

Truco
Spanish has upside-down exclamation and question marks at the beginning of sentences. Can you see some on this page? Try writing some! Does it feel strange?

Help your child: This unit is all about physical appearance with some guidelines on pronouns, verbs and how to express likes and dislikes. This will reinforce colour vocabulary while also introducing new adjectives. Encourage your child to use this new vocabulary to describe people in family photos or magazines.

Colorea el pelo y los ojos
Colour in the hair and eyes

VANESA

Mi pelo es negro y mis ojos son verdes.

JOSÉ

Mi pelo es castaño y mis ojos son verdes.

ALÍCIA

Mi pelo es rubio y mis ojos son marrones.

ALEJANDRO

Mi pelo es negro y mis ojos son marrones.

ADRIÁN

Mi pelo es pelirrojo y mis ojos son de color avellana.

MARÍA

Mi pelo es rubio y mis ojos son azules.

¡El detective!
Did you notice?

The verbs *es* and *son* were used in the exercise above. *Es* means *he/she/it is* and *son* means *they* <u>are</u>.

Mi pelo es rubio (My hair is blonde)

Mis ojos son marrones (My eyes are brown)

Diccionarito

mi pelo my hair
mis ojos my eyes
rubio blonde
castaño brown
negro black
pelirrojo red
rizado curly
liso straight
largo long
media melena mid-length
corto short
de color avellana hazel

¿Yo? Mi pelo es ....

y mis ....

¿Quién es?
Who is it?

ANTONIO

CARLA

MARTA

PABLO

SOFÍA

MARCOS

1. Tengo el pelo largo, liso y negro ....
2. Tengo el pelo negro, rubio y liso ....
3. Tengo el pelo negro y rizado ....
4. Tengo el pelo rizado y media melena ....
5. Tengo el pelo corto y castaño ....
6. Tengo el pelo rubio y liso ....

¡El detective!
Did you notice?

The word *tengo* was used a lot in the exercise above. It means 'I have'.
So why is it only one word?
In English, we often start sentences with I, you, she, he, it, we or they:

I have a sister, *we* eat dinner, *they* play tennis, *she* likes watching TV

These are called pronouns. But in Spanish the pronoun is often not
necessary. Instead you change the last few letters of the verb (the
doing word) to make it clear who is doing the action:

(yo)	tengo	I have
(tú)	tienes	you have
(él/ella)	tiene	he/she has

So we didn't need to say *yo tengo el pelo castaño* because *tengo* made it
clear who we were talking about – clever!
  Earlier we said that *es* means 'he/she/it is' and *son* means 'they are' –
again one word is enough to tell us who is speaking *and* what they're doing:

(yo)	soy	I am
(tú)	eres	you are
(él/ella)	es	he/she is
(ellos/ellas)	son	they are

Una pequeña historia: La familia de los camaleones
A little story: The chameleon family

Escucha y lee. Después pega las pegatinas en los espacios correctos
Listen and read. Then put the stickers in the correct places

Track 7

Soy el señor Camaleón.
I'm Mr Chameleon

Me encantan las moscas.
I love flies

¡Como muchas moscas!
I eat lots of flies!

¡Mira, soy verde como la hoja!
Look, I'm green like a leaf!

Soy la señora Camaleón.
I'm Mrs Chameleon

Me encantan las flores.
I love flowers

¡Qué bonita la flor rosa!
What a beautiful pink flower!

¡Mira, soy rosa como la flor!
Look, I'm pink like the flower!

Soy Clara Camaleón.
I'm Clara Chameleon.

Me encantan las mariposas.
I love butterflies.

¡Qué bonita la mariposa amarilla!
What a beautiful yellow butterfly!

¡Mira, soy amarilla como la mariposa!
Look, I'm yellow like the butterfly!

Diccionarito

como I eat
¡Mira! Look!
la flor flower
¡Qué bonito/a! How beautiful!
la mariposa butterfly
el nomeolvides forget-me-not
camuflado camouflaged
el saltamontes grasshopper
rico delicious

Soy Carolina Camaleón.
I'm Carolina Chameleon.

Me encantan los nomeolvides.
I love forget-me-nots.

¡Qué bonitas estas flores azules!
How beautiful these blue flowers are!

¡Mira, soy azul como el nomeolvides!
Look, I'm blue like the forget-me-not!

Soy Claudio Camaleón.
I'm Claudio Chameleon.

Estoy camuflado. Me escondo...
I'm camouflaged. I'm hiding...

Ah mira, un saltamontes. ¡Muy bien!
Oh look, a grasshopper. Oh good!

¡Me encantan los saltamontes!
I love grasshoppers!

Son muy ricos.
They're delicious.

¿Y tú?
And you?

¿Comes saltamontes?
Do you eat grasshoppers?

¡El detective!
Did you know?

When you really like something in Spanish, you say *me encanta.* If the thing you are talking about is plural, you add *-n* to the verb – *me encantan.*

Me encanta la flor amarilla (I love the yellow flower)
Me encantan las flores amarillas (I love the yellow flowers)

Literally, it means 'yellow flowers enchant me'.

¡FELIZ CUMPLEAÑOS!

5. Happy birthday!

Help your child: This unit is designed to help your child talk about birthdays, thus covering months of the year and numbers up to 31, plus pronunciation of vowels. Your child does not need to learn how to write all these numbers at this stage but seeing them written as words helps pronunciation. Encourage the use of this new vocabulary to practise vowel sounds.

Mi cumpleaños
My birthday

 once

 doce

 trece

 catorce

 quince

 dieciséis

 diecisiete

 dieciocho

 diecinueve

 veinte

> **Truco**
> Remember to pronounce the last part of numbers 11-15 with a *th* sound as in 'thumb'.

> **Truco**
> Numbers 16-19 follow a pattern. The direct translation would be ten-and-six, ten-and-seven...

¡El detective!
Did you notice?

Numbers above twenty are easy in Spanish. You know that 'twenty' is *veinte* so, to get to thirty, change *veinte* to *veinti* and add numbers 1-9 to the end:

21	22	23	24	25
veintiuno	veintidós	veintitrés	veinticuatro	veinticinco

26	27	28	29
veintiséis	veintisiete	veintiocho	veintinueve

Numbers from 30 are almost the same except they are written as separate words with *y* (which means 'and') in the middle:

treinta y uno 31 (thirty and one)   *treinta y dos* 32 (thirty and two)

Los meses del año

Months of the year

Escribe los meses en el orden correcto
Write the months in the correct order

mayo ..4...   octubre ..10.   julio ..7....   septiembre ..9...

febrero ..2..   junio ..6...   enero ..1...   diciembre ..12

agosto ..8...   marzo ..3...   abril ..5...   noviembre ..11...

Truco

Most of the months are very like their English equivalents. January is the most different, so we've done that one for you.

Truco

In Spanish the months don't need a capital letter.

Rellena las casillas y encuentra una palabra nueva en la columna vertical
Fill in the grid to find a new word in the vertical column

1. the shortest month of the year
2. the month before *diciembre*
3. the month after *julio*
4. the third month of the year
5. the month after *junio*
6. the fifth month of the year
7. the Spanish word for 'months'

The word that is spelled out
is something everyone likes to receive
lots of on their birthday – presents!

..r e g a l o...

f	e	b	r	e	r	o
n	o	v	i	e	m	b	r	e
		a	g	o	s	t	o
		m	a	r	z	o
		j	u	l	i	o
	M	a	y	o
		M	e	s	e	s

¡El detective!

Did you know?

In English, vowels (a, e, i, o, u) can change their sound depending on where they are: *a* sounds different in 'apple', 'ate' and 'ball'. But in Spanish they always sound the same so reading should be easier than in many other languages.

The CD will help you to find the right pronunciation.

Dibuja las velas en los pasteles
Draw the candles on the cakes

Truco
To say how old you are in Spanish, you say 'I have ... years'.

¿Cuántos años tienes?
How old are you?

¿Cuándo es tu cumpleaños?
When is your birthday?

1. Tengo nueve años.
I'm nine years old.

Mi cumpleaños
es el 11 de julio.
My birthday is on 11th July.

2. Tengo dieciséis años.

Mi cumpleaños es
el 7 de septiembre.

3. Tengo siete años.
Mi cumpleaños
es el 25 de octubre.

4. Tengo quince años.
Mi cumpleaños es
el 8 de mayo.

5. Tengo ocho años.
Mi cumpleaños
es el 22 de febrero.

¿Y tú? ¿Cuántos años tienes?

Tengo .... años.

¿Cuándo es tu cumpleaños?

Mi cumpleaños es el .... de ....

Truco
Try singing Happy Birthday in Spanish. They use the same tune as we do in English.

Diccionarito

¡Cumpleaños feliz! Happy birthday! (literally: birthday happy)
¡Cumpleaños feliz! Happy birthday!
Te deseamos todos We all wish you
¡Cumpleaños feliz! Happy birthday!

¡El detective!
Did you notice?

There is a funny symbol above the *n* in *año*. This is because the Spanish alphabet has some extra letters! Just imagine there is a *y* after the *n*, as in the girl's name 'Tan*y*a'.

Practise saying *año, cumpleaños, pequeño/a, castaño/a, español, España...*

¿QUÉ HORA ES?

6. What time is it?

I II III IV V VI VII VIII IX X XI XII

Help your child: In this unit, your child will learn how to tell the time and to say the days of the week. Studying the time will also provide an opportunity for some revision of numbers. Encourage your child to begin to talk about their daily life to practise the days of the week – and try asking them for the time in Spanish from now on!

Dibuja las manecillas en los relojes
Draw the hands on the clocks

Son las cinco

Son las dos

Es la una

Son las ocho

Son las once

Son las cuatro

¡El detective!
Did you notice?

When we are talking about lots of things (eye<u>s</u>, kite<u>s</u>), el changes to los and *la* to *las*. This is called the plural.

	masculine	**feminine**	
singular	*el ojo*	*la cometa*	(the eye / the kite)
plural	*los ojos*	*las cometas*	(the eyes / the kites)

¡El detective!
Did you notice?

Spanish uses *son las* and a number to say 'it's ... o'clock' but for 1 o'clock they use *es la una*. The rest is easy!

```
                          12
menos cinco  11                        1  y cinco
menos diez  10                         2  y diez
menos cuarto  9            ·            3  y cuarto
menos veinte  8                        4  y veinte
menos veinticinco  7                   5  y veinticinco
                           6
                        y media
```

Son las cinco y cuarto	It's quarter past five (*literally: It's five and quarter*)
Son las siete y media	It's half past seven (*literally: It's seven and half*)
Son las tres menos cuarto	It's quarter to three (*literally: It's three minus quarter*)
Son las cuatro y diez	It's ten past four (*literally: It's four and ten*)
Son las nueve menos veinticinco	It's twenty-five to nine (*literally: It's nine minus twenty-five*)

Traduce las frases
Translate the sentences

It's twenty past two ....

It's quarter to seven ....

It's five to five ....

It's half past eleven ....

It's twenty to one ....

¿Qué hora es ahora?
What time is it now?

....

Completa las frases
Complete the sentences

Desayuno a las ....   I have breakfast at ....

Voy a la escuela a las ....   I go to school at ....

Almuerzo a la(s) ....   I have lunch at ....

Voy a casa a las ....   I go home at ....

Ceno a las ....   I have dinner at ....

Los días de la semana
Days of the week

Relaciona los días en español con los días en inglés
Match the days in Spanish with the days in English

lunes	Wednesday
martes	Friday
miércoles	Tuesday
jueves	Saturday
viernes	Monday
sábado	Sunday
domingo	Thursday

Una rima: Escucha y participa
A rhyme: Listen and join in

Track 8

Completa los días de la semana en español
Complete the days of the week in Spanish

Los l ..... n ..... s canto en el coro
On Mondays I sing in the choir

Los ..... a ..... t ..... s voy al laboratorio
On Tuesdays I go to the lab

Los m ..... ér ..... o ..... es tengo inglés
On Wednesdays I have English

Los ..... u ..... v ..... s estudio francés
On Thursdays I study French

Los v ..... e ..... n ..... s suena la campana
On Fridays the bell rings

¡Por fin, es el fin de semana!
Finally, it's the weekend!

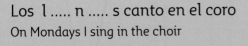

De Pies a Cabeza

7. From head to toe

Help your child: This unit covers vocabulary for parts of the body and introduces some new verbs. There is also some revision of numbers, colours and masculine/feminine nouns. Encourage your child to point to parts of their own body and name them.

Truco
In Spanish, you say 'from feet to head' instead of 'from head to toe'.

Une las palabras con la parte correcta del cuerpo
Draw a line linking the words to the correct part of the body

la cabeza
head

los ojos
eyes

los dientes
teeth

la nariz
nose

las orejas
ears

la boca
mouth

el brazo
arm

los dedos
fingers/toes

la mano
hand

la barriga
tummy

el pie
foot

la pierna
leg

Escribe las partes del cuerpo en español
Write the parts of the body in Spanish

finger/toe ....

tummy ....

mouth ....

foot ....

hand ....

arm ....

head ....

nose ....

ear ....

eye ....

leg ....

tooth ....

el

la

Ahora relaciona las palabras con "el" o "la"
Now match the words with el or la

Relaciona las frases
Match the phrases

Escucho ...

Huelo ...

Como ...

Miro ...

Toco ...

Camino ...

Llevo guantes ...

Llevo calcetines ...

Llevo un sombrero ...

con los ojos

en los pies

con las orejas

en la cabeza

con la nariz

en las manos

con las piernas

con los dedos

con la boca

Truco
Spanish uses the same word for fingers and toes! You say *dedos de la mano* (fingers of the hand) or *dedos del pie* (fingers of the foot) to mark the difference.

Diccionarito
con with
en on/in
escucho I listen
huelo I smell
como I eat
miro I look
toco I touch
camino I walk
llevo I wear
guantes gloves
calcetines socks

¡El detective!
Did you notice?

When talking about the body in Spanish, you don't normally use 'my' like we do in English - use 'the' instead:

Escucho con <u>las</u> orejas — I listen with my ears (*literally: I listen with <u>the</u> ears*)

Tengo <u>las</u> manos frías — My hands are cold (*literally: I have <u>the</u> hands cold*)

Mira el monstruo y escribe la palabra correcta en el hueco

Look at the monster and write the correct word in each space

¡Hola! ¿Qué tal? Me llamo Miguel el

Monstruo. Tengo .... cabezas,

cinco .... , una

.... , ... ojos,

.........................narices, ...

orejas y una boca.

Ahora colorea el monstruo y completa la frase

Now colour in the monster and complete the sentence

¿De qué color es Miguel?

What colour is Miguel?

Miguel el Monstruo es ....

Dibuja tu propio monstruo y rellena el globo

Now draw your own monster and fill in the speech balloon

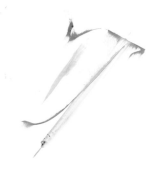

¡Hola! ¿Qué tal?

Me llamo .... el Monstruo.

Tengo ....

....

....

Canción: Escucha y canta

Song: Listen and sing

Track 9

Una hora andando, andando, andando,
One hour of walking, walking, walking,

Una hora andando se agotan los pies.
One hour of walking, it wears out your feet.

Dos horas andando ...

Escribe las letras en el orden correcto

Write the letters in the correct order

jreao ....

aaigrrb ....

arzob ....

zabeca ....

entied ....

Truco
Can you remember what all of these words mean? If you've forgotten, look them up in a dictionary.

Sopa de letras: ¿Cuántas partes del cuerpo puedes encontrar?

Word search: How many parts of the body can you find?

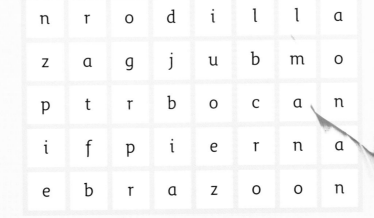

n	r	o	d	i	l	l	a
z	a	g	j	u	b	m	o
p	t	r	b	o	c	a	n
i	f	p	i	e	r	n	a
e	b	r	a	z	o	o	n

MI ROPA

Hecho en España

8. My clothes

Help your child: In this unit your child will learn to describe what they are wearing. This also incorporates more practice of gender and colours. Using family photos, you can encourage extra practice. If an item of clothing is not mentioned in the book, help your child to look up the word in a dictionary or online at www.collinslanguage.com.

En el circo: Escucha y participa
At the circus: Listen and join in

Track 10

Un domador y un tambor
A tamer and a drum

Una carpa y una caravana
A big top and a caravan

Un cañón y un león
A cannon and a lion

Una corbata y una acróbata
A tie and an acrobat

Un guante y un elefante
A glove and an elephant

Una chaqueta y una bicicleta
A jacket and a bike

Un trapecista y un jefe de pista
A trapeze artist and a ringmaster

Una malabarista y una equilibrista
A juggler and a tightrope walker

Un zapato y un gato
A shoe and a cat

Un monociclo y un triciclo
A unicycle and a tricycle

Un mago y un payaso
A magician and a clown

Un músico y un látigo.
A musician and a whip.

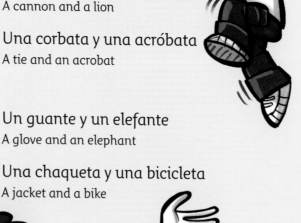

Completa el texto con "un" o "una" y colorea la imagen
Complete the text with un or una and colour in the picture

El payaso lleva .... pantalón verde,

.... chaqueta roja, ... camisa azul,

.... corbata amarilla, ... sombrero

negro, ... flor blanca, ... paraguas rosa

y dos enormes zapatos marrones.

Colorea la ropa y escribe el color en el hueco
Colour in the clothes and then write in the colour in the space

un pijama ....

unos pantalones cortos ....

una camiseta de fútbol ....

un vestido amarillo

una camiseta roja

una camisa morada

una sudadera ....

unos tejanos ....

un pantalón marrón

una falda rosa

un jersey azul

Diccionarito
el paraguas umbrella
la flor flower
el payaso clown
la chaqueta jacket
el zapato shoe
la corbata tie
el pantalón/los pantalones trousers
la camisa shirt
los guantes gloves

Truco
Remember that all colours have to agree with what they're describing. Did you put the correct ending on each word?

The word *unos* was used with *tejanos* (jeans) and *pantalones cortos* (shorts).
These are plural words so you have to make *un* and *una* plural to match.

un – unos	*una – unas*
un vestido – unos vestidos	a dress – some dresses
una falda – unas faldas	a skirt – some skirts

Diccionarito

las bambas trainers
los zapatos shoes
las botas boots
las botas de goma wellington boots
las zapatillas slippers

Pega las pegatinas en el espacio correcto

Stick the stickers in the right spaces

unas bambas blancas

unos zapatos negros

unas bambas verdes

unas botas marrones

unas botas de goma rosas

unas zapatillas blancas

Relaciona las palabras españolas con las palabras inglesas

Match the Spanish words with the English words

unas bambas	shirt
una camisa	trainers
unos tejanos	skirt
una falda	dress
un jersey	football shirt
una camiseta de fútbol	pyjamas
un pantalón	trousers
un pijama	jumper
un vestido	jeans

Truco
Did you notice the word *pijama*? It's almost the same as in English but in Spanish it's singular. The Spanish word for trousers can be singular or plural.

cinco

siete

diez

tres

seis

dos

Relaciona las descripciones con las imágenes. Después coloréalas

Match the descriptions to the pictures. Then colour in each picture

SOFÍA

PABLO

1. Llevo mis pantalones negros, mi camiseta roja y mis bambas blancas.

2. Llevo mi camiseta de fútbol, mis pantalones cortos negros y mis bambas negras.

3. Llevo mi vestido verde, mi sombrero amarillo y los zapatos de mi madre.

4. Llevo mi sudadera rosa, mis tejanos negros y mis bambas moradas.

MARTA

ANTONIO

Mi Habitación

9. My bedroom

Help your child: This unit will help your child learn about bedroom vocabulary and prepositions of place. Encourage your child to describe different bedrooms in your home. Using numbers, colours and other adjectives we have covered will make the descriptions much more interesting. With longer texts like these it is also worth remembering that in foreign languages it is not necessary to understand every word. If your child can get the gist, that is the first step.

Lee el texto y escribe los colores en los espacios
Read the text and write the colours in the spaces

En mi habitación hay una cama ....,
un armario .... y una mesilla
de noche .... al lado de la cama. Hay
una lámpara .... encima. Hay un
escritorio .... y tiene una silla
.... al lado. Hay una alfombra
.... Mi habitación tiene muchos
colores. ¡Me encanta!

¡El detective!
Did you notice?

Spanish uses the word *hay* (pronounced like the English word 'eye') to say 'there is' or 'there are'. Unlike in English, it is always the same whether you are referring to plural or singular:

there is .... *hay*
there are ....

Diccionarito

la cama bed
el armario wardrobe
la mesilla de noche bedside table
al lado (de) beside
la lámpara lamp
encima on top
escritorio desk
silla chair
la alfombra rug

Canción: Lee y canta. Después pega las pegatinas en el espacio correcto
Song: Read and sing along. Then put the stickers in the correct place

Track 11

Tengo un gatito.
I have a kitten.

Es muy bonito.
It's very beautiful.

Caza ratoncitos.
It catches mice.

¿Dónde estás, gatito bonito?
Where are you, beautiful kittie?

¡Miau, miau! ¡Miau, miau!
Miaow, miaow! Miaow, miaow!

Estoy debajo de la cama.
I'm under the bed.

Estoy debajo de la cama.
I'm under the bed.

Diccionarito
debajo de under
encima de on top of
dentro de in, inside

Tengo un gatito.

Es muy bonito.

Caza ratoncitos.

¿Dónde estás, gatito bonito?

¡Miau, miau! ¡Miau, miau!

Estoy encima de la cama.
I'm on the bed.

Estoy encima de la cama.
I'm on the bed.

Tengo un gatito.

Es muy bonito.

Caza ratoncitos.

¿Dónde estás, gatito bonito?

¡Miau, miau! ¡Miau, miau!

Estoy dentro de la cama.
I'm in the bed!

¡Miau, miau! ¡Miau, miau!

¡Shhhh! Estoy durmiendo.
Shhhh! I'm sleeping!

¡Buenas noches!
Good night!

¡El detective!

Did you notice?

The kitten says _estoy encima de la cama._ I'm on the bed. Why is it _estoy_?
There are two words for 'be' in Spanish. _Ser_ is used for things that are
permanent and _estar_ for location and things that aren't permanent.

     ser – be (in a permanent state)

     (yo) soy   I am

     (tú) eres   you are

     (él/ella) es   he/she is

     estar – be (in a temporary state or for location)

     (yo) estoy   I am

     (tú) estás   you are

     (él/ella) está he/she is

In the kitten song, _ser_ is used (**es** _muy bonito_) because the kitten is _always_
beautiful and _estar_ is used (_¿Dónde_ **estás**? and **estoy** _debajo/encima/dentro
de la cama_) to say where or how the cat is _at the moment._

Which is true? Underline the correct answer.

In Spanish, you say...

1. a) (Yo) soy en la cama. b) (Yo) estoy en la cama.

2. a) ¿Dónde está?   b) ¿Dónde es?

Mira las imágenes y completa las frases. Después colorea las imágenes

Look at the pictures and complete the sentences. Then colour in the pictures

El ratoncito está encima del . . . .

. . . . ratoncito está debajo del sombrero.

El . . . . está dentro del sombrero.

¡El ratoncito come el sombrero!

38 Mi habitación

Poema: Lee en voz alta

Poem: Read out loud

En mi casa hay un jardín

At my house there is a garden

¿Un jardín?

A garden?

Sí, un jardín. Y en el jardín hay un árbol.

Yes, a garden. And in the garden there is a tree.

¿Un árbol?

A tree?

Sí, un árbol. Y en el árbol hay una rama.

Yes, a tree. And in the tree there is a branch.

¿Una rama?

A branch?

Sí, una rama. Y en la rama hay un nido.

Yes, a branch. And on the branch there is a nest.

¿Un nido?

A nest?

Sí, un nido. Y en el nido hay un huevo.

Yes, a nest. And in the nest there is an egg.

¿Un huevo?

An egg?

Sí, un huevo. Y en el huevo hay...

Yes, an egg. And in the egg there is...

¿Qué hay?

What is there?

Hay un pajarito.

There is a little bird.

¡Qué bonito el pajarito!

What a cute little bird!

10. My things

Help your child: This unit introduces school objects and some basic verbs. Colour vocabulary, masculine/feminine, singular/plural nouns and possessives are also revisited. Help your child to name the objects in their schoolbag and pencil case and to talk a little about school. Join in with the fun rap at the end!

Pega las pegatinas en el espacio correcto
Stick the stickers in the correct spaces

las tijeras   la cola   los libros de texto   los cuadernos

la goma   el lápiz   la regla   el bolígrafo   los rotuladores

¿Qué hay en el estuche? Escribe las letras en el orden correcto
What's in the pencil case? Write the letters in the correct order

páliz ....

fagíbloro ....

lagre ....

moag ....

rajetis ....

Truco
Do the ones you know first and see what you have left.

Diccionarito
la cartera schoolbag
el estuche pencil case
los lápices de colores coloured pencils

Escribe los colores de los lápices
Write the colours of the pencils

....

....

....

....

....

¿Cuántos lápices de colores hay en el estuche?
How many coloured pencils are there in the pencil case?

There are ten coloured pencils in the pencil case.

H a y .... l á p i c e s ....

.... e n ....

Truco
Remember *mi* and *mis* both mean 'my'. *Mi* is used before singular nouns and *mis* before plural nouns.

Completa las frases con "mi" o "mis"
Complete the sentences with *mi* or *mis*

En .... cartera hay .... cuadernos, ...

libros de texto, ... estuche y .... bambas.

En .... estuche hay .... bolígrafo, ... lápices, ...

rotuladores, ... goma, ... cola y ....tijeras.

El abecedario
The alphabet

Escucha y participa
Listen and join in

Track 13

A de azul

B de bota

C de cabra

CH de chimpancé

D de día

E de elefante

F de febrero

G de guante

H de hoja

I de inglés

J de jirafa

K de kilómetro

L de libro

LL de gallo

M de mano

N de noviembre

Ñ de año

O de ojo

P de perro

Q de queso

R de rojo

S de sombrero

T de tigre

U de uno

V de vestido

W de web

X de xilófono

Y de yo-yo

Z de zoo

Truco

Did you notice the three letters that don't appear in the English alphabet? They are *ch*, *ll* and *ñ*. Listen carefully to the CD to hear how they are pronounced.

azul

lunes
martes

kilómetro

brero

noviembre

inglés

Resumen

Summary

Escoge la(s) palabra(s) correcta(s) para completar las frases
Choose the correct word(s) to complete the sentences

la   pronoun   I am

y   unos

mis

masculine   unas

yellow   el

una   accent

th   differently

days

feminine   Months

un

mi   thumb

1. I know that all nouns in Spanish are either .... or ....

2. The word for 'the' before a singular noun is .... or ....

3. A lot of Spanish words are related to English words but are pronounced
....

4. In Spanish, you normally stress the second from last syllable or the syllable with an ....

5. The words for 'a' are .... or ....

6. *Soy* and *estoy* both mean ....

7. The word for 'my' is .... before singular nouns and .... before plural nouns.

8. To say 'some', you use .... or ....

9. .... and .... don't need a capital letter in Spanish.

10. Spanish speakers often leave out the .... before the verb.

11. In Spanish, *ll* is pronounced like the .... in ....

12. *ce* is pronounced like .... in ....

Answer key

Pg 4

el canguro
el león
el hipopótamo
la jirafa
el chimpancé
el elefante
el cocodrilo

el = león, canguro,
elefante, cocodrilo,
chimpancé, tigre,
hipopótamo
la = cebra, tortuga, jirafa

Pg 5

Word search
cocodrilo
canguro
león
tigre
cebra
jirafa
elefante
tortuga

Which is true?
1. B. the *th* in thirty
2. A. *ce* and *ci* sound the
   same as the Spanish *z*
3. A. the *ch* in the Scottish
   word loch
4. B. *ge* and *gi* sound the
   same as the Spanish *j*

Pg 7

7 = siete
2 = dos
6 = seis
10 = diez
5 = cinco
3 = tres

Clockwise from top right:
siete huesos (7), cuatro
huesos (4), nueve huesos
(9), tres huesos (3), ocho
huesos (8)

Which is true?
1. B. the *y* in yellow
2. A. the *r* in 'brrrrr, it's
   cold!'

Pg 8

Nueve vacas
siete pollitos
ocho burritos
seis conejos
diez cabras

Pg 9

granja gato conejo jirafa
cebra cinco chimpancé
  cabra
pollo caballo cocodrilo
  gallo

Pg 11

Carla = red & yellow
Antonio = blue & green
Pablo = black & white
Marta = pink & grey
Sofía = green & red
Marcos = blue & yellow

Pg 12

una manzana roja
un elefante gris
una jirafa amarilla
  (y marrón)
un sombrero azul
una mariposa verde
un gato negro

Pg 13

*Poem: using words from
the diccionarito*
Negro como la noche,
Blanco como la nieve,
Rojo como un tomate,
Azul como el mar,
Amarillo como el sol,
Verde como una hoja.

Pg 14

Vanesa has black hair and
  green eyes
José has brown hair and
  green eyes
Alícia has blonde hair and
  brown eyes
Alejandro has black hair
  and brown eyes
Adrián has red hair and
  hazel eyes
María has blonde hair and
  blue eyes

Pg 15

1. Marta
2. Antonio
3. Carla
4. Sofía
5. Pablo
6. Marcos

Pg 19

mayo 5
octubre 10
julio 7
septiembre 9
febrero 2
junio 6
enero 1
diciembre 12
agosto 8
marzo 3
abril 4
noviembre 11

1. febrero
2. noviembre
3. agosto
4. marzo
5. julio

6. mayo
7. meses
The word that is spelled
out is 'regalos'

Pg 20

1. 9 years old
2. 16 years old
3. 7 years old
4. 15 years old
5. 8 years old

Pg 25

5 o'clock
2 o'clock
1 o'clock
8 o'clock
11 o'clock
4 o'clock

Pg 26

Son las dos y veinte
Son las siete menos cuarto
Son las cinco menos cinco
Son las once y media
Es la una menos veinte

Pg 27

lunes = Monday
martes = Tuesday
miércoles = Wednesday
jueves = Thursday
viernes = Friday
sábado = Saturday
domingo = Sunday

Los lunes canto en el coro,
Los martes voy al
  laboratorio,
Los miércoles tengo inglés,
Los jueves estudio francés,
Los viernes suena la
  campana,
¡Por fin, es el fin de
  semana!

Pg 29

el = dedo, pie, brazo, ojo,
  diente
la = barriga, boca, mano,
  cabeza, nariz, oreja, pierna

Escucho con las orejas
  (I listen with my ears)
huelo con la nariz
  (I smell with my nose)
como con la boca
  (I eat with my mouth)
miro con los ojos
  (I look with my eyes)
toco con los dedos
  (I touch with my fingers)
camino con las piernas
  (I walk with my legs)
llevo guantes en las manos
  (I wear gloves on my
  hands)
llevo calcetines en los pies

  (I wear socks on my feet)
llevo un sombrero en la
  cabeza (I wear a hat on
  my head)

Pg 30

¡Hola! ¿Qué tal? Me llamo
  Miguel el Monstruo.
Tengo tres cabezas, cinco
  brazos, una pierna, nueve
  ojos, cuatro narices, seis
  orejas y una boca.

Pg 31

oreja
barriga
brazo
cabeza
diente

Word search
pierna
pie
boca
brazo
rodilla
ojo
mano
nariz

Pg 33

El payaso lleva un pantalón
  verde, una chaqueta roja,
  una camisa azul, una
  corbata amarilla, un
  sombrero negro, una flor
  blanca, un paraguas rosa,
  y dos enormes zapatos
  marrones.

un pijama azul
unos pantalones cortos
  rojos
una camiseta de fútbol
  naranja
un vestido amarillo *(yellow)*
unos tejanos azules
una camiseta roja *(red)*
un pantalón marrón
  (brown)
una camisa morada
  (purple)
una falda rosa *(pink)*
una sudadera verde
un jersey azul *(blue)*

Pg 34

unas bambas = trainers
una camisa = shirt
unos tejanos = jeans
una falda = skirt
un jersey = jumper
una camiseta de fútbol
  = football shirt
un pantalón = trousers
un pijama = pyjamas
un vestido = dress

Pg 35

1. Antonio
2. Pablo
3. Marta
4. Sofía

Pg 36

En mi habitación hay una
cama azul, un armario
marrón y una mesilla de
noche naranja al lado de
la cama. Hay una lámpara
negra encima. Hay un
escritorio rojo y tiene una
silla roja al lado. Hay una
alfombra amarilla. Mi
habitación tiene muchos
colores. ¡Me encanta!

Pg 38

Which is true?
1. B. (Yo) estoy en la cama
2. A. ¿Dónde está?

El ratoncito está encima
  del sombrero
El ratoncito está debajo
  del sombrero
El ratoncito está dentro
  del sombrero.

Pg 40

lápiz, regla, tijeras,
bolígrafo, goma

Pg 41

rojo, amarillo, verde, azul,
rosa, morado, marrón,
negro, gris, naranja

Hay diez lápices de colores
en el estuche.

En mi cartera hay mis
cuadernos, mis libros de
texto, mi estuche y mis
bambas.
En mi estuche hay mi
bolígrafo, mis lápices, mis
rotuladores, mi goma, mi
cola y mis tijeras.

Resumen

1. masculine, feminine
2. el, la
3. differently
4. accent
5. un, una
6. I am
7. mi, mis
8. unos, unas
9. Months, days
10. pronoun
11. y, yellow
12. th, thumb